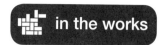
in the works

D1241712

What Do I Do With My Life?

SERVING GOD THROUGH WORK

Kenneth A. Baker

FAITH ALIVE®
Christian Resources

Grand Rapids, Michigan

Photo: iStock

This study is part of In the Works, a faith formation program for adults.

Studies in this series include:
Where Do I Come In? Joining God's Mission
What Do I Do with My Life? Serving God through Work
What Do I Owe? Managing the Gifts God Gives You
How Do I Make It Right? Doing Justice in a Broken World?
How Do I Begin? Sharing Your Faith

What Do I Do with My Life? Serving God through Work, © 2010 by Faith Alive Christian Resources, 2850 Kalamazoo Ave. SE, Grand Rapids, MI 49560. All rights reserved. With the exception of brief excerpts for review purposes, no part of this book may be reproduced in any manner whatsoever without written permission from the publisher. Printed in the United States of America.

We welcome your comments. Call us at 1-800-333-8300 or e-mail us at editors@faithaliveresources.org.

ISBN 978-1-59255-471-3

10 9 8 7 6 5 4 3 2 1

Contents

How to Use This Book

What Do I Do with My Life? Serving God through Work, as well as the other books in the In the Works series, offers a unique format that combines insightful daily devotions with a discussion guide for small groups. It's simple and easy to use. Here's all you need to do:

Before your group meeting, please carefully read the five daily readings that offer insights on the topic for the week. You'll find them stimulating and full of practical ways to help you serve God in your workplace. We suggest reading one devotional on each of the five days rather than reading through all five at once. That way you can take your time and reflect on what the reading says to you personally. You may want to highlight lines that speak to you or jot questions or comments in the margin.

Note: Before your first small group session, you should have received a copy of this book so you can read the daily readings for Week 1 prior to your first meeting.

During your group meeting, use the small group discussion guides found at the end of each week of readings. These self-directing guides offer plenty to talk about for forty-five minutes to an hour or more. Groups should feel free to use them selectively, choosing the questions or activities that fit the group and the amount of time you have.

Each discussion guide includes

- an **Opening** question or activity that takes group members into the topic for the session.
- a **Bible Study** of passages that relate to the topic of the week. Group members should bring their own Bibles to the meetings or arrange to have a supply of Bibles available.
- **Group Discussion** questions that take participants back into the daily readings for the week and help relate them to their daily lives. Groups should feel free to select which

of these questions they want to discuss; of course, you can always substitute questions and comments from group members for our precooked ones!

- a brief **Closing** time of focus and prayer.
- **Action Options** for groups and for individuals. These are suggestions for follow-up activities that flow from the daily readings and group discussion.

From time to time, the discussion guides offer **Options** or **Alternative Approaches**, giving groups a choice of activities or questions.

In addition, the weekly discussion guides in this book include **Case Studies** and follow-up discussion questions that relate to each week's theme. If you decide to use them, you should be aware that you'll have less time for the discussion questions that follow.

Of course you'll want someone who's willing to lead the discussion and keep things moving for each small group meeting. But the discussion guide is written for the whole group, not just the leader. Together, may you grow in your understanding of how to participate with Christ in redeeming and restoring your workplaces.

—Faith Alive staff

Introduction

For most adult Christians in North America the workplace is the *primary* arena for practicing discipleship. It is the world we enter daily. Assuming a career of forty years and an average workweek of fifty hours, we will spend over one hundred thousand hours in the workplace before retirement! By comparison, even the most active church member will devote only about five thousand hours to "church activity" over that same forty-year period. For most adult Christians in North America, the workplace is our primary arena for practicing discipleship.

Let that sink in—for every hour we are called to follow Jesus in church activity, we are called to follow him for over twenty hours in our occupations as trash collectors, corporate CEOs, small business owners, assembly line workers, middle managers, farmers, truck drivers, teachers, accountants, homemakers, students, or volunteers in the community.

Ordinarily we use the word *work* to refer to formal employment or wage-earning jobs. But that leaves too many people out of the equation—retirees, homemakers, children, students, and volunteers. So in this study we'll be using Paul Marshall's broader definition of work as "any effort to shape and influence the world around us, including other people" (*Heaven Is Not My Home*).

When it comes to not merely listening to God's Word but doing what it says (James 1:22), the workplace is where our faith takes active shape. It is where Jesus asks us to "love the Lord your God with all your heart and with all your soul and with all your mind and with all your strength" and to "love your neighbor as yourself" (Mark 12:33). It is where we "continue to work out [our] salvation with fear and trembling" (Philippians 2:12). It is where we must translate Sunday's good news into weekday action. Our workplace offers the greatest opportunity to exert influence as the "salt of the earth" and the "light of the world" (Matthew 5:13, 14).

This study guide invites you to explore what it means to follow Christ in the workplace, whatever that workplace might be. In personal reflection and small group discussion you will discover what God's Word teaches about your high calling to serve and represent the Lord every day when you go to work.

Kingdom Work

MAY THE WORDS OF MY
MOUTH AND THE MEDITATIONS
OF MY HEART BE PLEASING
IN YOUR SIGHT, MY ROCK
AND REDEEMER.
PSALMS

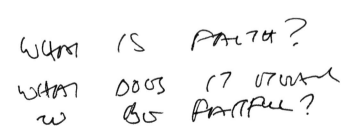

WHAT IS FAITH?
WHAT DOES IT MEAN
TO BE FAITHFUL?

Called to Ministry

So God created human beings in his own image. . . .
God blessed them and said to them, "Be fruitful and
increase in number; fill the earth and subdue it."
—*Genesis 1:27, 28*

'm a pastor. I have two sons in seminary preparing to go into "the ministry." I have a daughter who teaches cognitively impaired children in a public school. I love telling people what my kids do. The typical response is something like, "That's wonderful! You must be so proud!"

In my church we conduct "ordination" services for elders, deacons, ministry associates, and ministers of the Word. We "install" these persons into their respective "offices." We call them *officebearers*. In our ordination forms we ask them if they feel "called" by God in the call of the congregation. We also "commission" other church workers, including Sunday school teachers and people who represent us on a mission trip, and talk about the valuable "ministry" they perform.

These same persons may devote twenty, forty, or more hours every week to their work as business owners, construction workers, managers, plumbers, homemakers, or Hospice volunteers. Ordinarily, though, we do not ask them whether they feel called to such work. We do not set them apart, commission them, or honor the office they hold in the workplace during the week. We don't offer special prayers or thank the Lord for their ministry in the workplace. When we hear of a son or daughter of the congregation who is heading for seminary or going on a mission trip, it stirs a sense of pride and communal joy among us that is not quite matched by word of a young adult heading for nursing school or working for a lawn care service for the summer.

Why do you suppose that is?

It's no wonder many people are inclined to think of *work* in two categories—secular work and "kingdom" work. They somehow feel that there must be a difference between working "for the Lord" and just having a job. Some struggle in the midst of successful careers with whether they should make a change and go into "full-time ministry."

This tension is not surprising. Ever since the Middle Ages, Christians have been strangely drawn to the two-story view of life that elevates church work ("ministry") above secular work. Back then most people thought of the ideal Christian life as living in a monastery, devoting all your time to meditation, prayer, and worship. The Protestant Reformers shattered this perspective by recovering the biblical concept of *calling* (or vocation) as rooted in the biblical account of creation.

The opening chapter of the Bible teaches that we humans are created in God's image. God gave all of us a job to do: to "fill the earth and subdue it"; to "rule over" his kingdom of creation (Genesis 1:28). We'll explore this further in Week 2. For now it is enough to recognize that this calling extends to *all* we do to care for and unfold God's creation. This is the calling or vocation of every Christ-follower, regardless of our particular occupation.

That means *every* job is "ministry" for a disciple of Christ!

The Disciple's Ruling Passion

"But seek first his kingdom and his righteousness,
and all these things will be given to you as well."
—Matthew 6:33

I love the Olympics. But personally I'd be happy if we eliminated "dream teams" stocked with millionaire professionals and stuck with amateurs. I prefer to follow the story of some sixteen-year-old gymnast from Idaho or Nova Scotia who has made countless sacrifices for years in order to pursue a dream of competing in the games. The single-minded passion of these athletes is remarkable. It drives them, consumes them, and stirs them to an amazing level of dedication and performance.

Jesus calls us to the same single-minded passion in the words at the top of this page. *"Seek first [God's] kingdom and his righteousness. . . ."* In the language of the New Testament, *seek* is a strong word. It means to strive, to search for or attempt earnestly. On top of that it's a command word. And as if that were not enough emphasis, he adds the adverb *first*, that is, above all!

So Jesus isn't suggesting here a course of action as an option for us to try and see how it works for us. He is calling us to embrace this as a compelling pursuit, to go after it with a single-minded passion, to make it our foremost priority. "Above all else," he's saying, "immerse yourselves in the pursuit of expressing the reign of God more fully in your lives and in your world."

This is the commission and mission of every disciple of Christ. And because the reign of God extends over *all* areas of life, it's true also in the workplace. Like athletes consumed by a dream of competing in the Olympic games, Christ wants us to be consumed by the dream of seeing the places we work shaped by the values of his kingdom—values like justice, fairness, equity, goodness, and mercy.

As disciples of Christ, this pursuit should be the one that motivates us above all others when we get up in the morning and get ready for work. Not the pursuit of wealth or status or personal advancement, but the pursuit of God's kingdom. This passion and pursuit shapes *all* of our work—church work, home work, volunteer work, or occupational work. It makes *all* of our work "kingdom work"!

Filled with the Spirit

"See, I have chosen Bezalel son of Uri . . . and I have filled
him with the Spirit of God . . . to make artistic designs
for work in gold, silver and bronze, to cut and set stones,
to work in wood, and to engage in all kinds of crafts."
—*Exodus 31:2-5*

I recently counseled someone who was feeling distressed about her relationship to God. According to the church she'd been attending, the mark of being saved is to be "filled with the Spirit," and the evidence of being filled is the ability to speak in tongues. She had always considered her faith in Christ to be genuine, but now she was unsure that she was really saved because even though she prayed for it, she did not receive the gift of tongues.

What comes to mind when you think of Paul's command to "be filled with the Spirit" (Ephesians 5:18)? Are there people in your life that you consider to be Spirit-filled? How about you? Do you consider yourself to be Spirit-filled? What suggests that someone is filled with the Spirit? Is it the depth of her prayer life? The fervor with which she worships on Sundays? The number of committees or programs at church in which she serves? Or perhaps the ability to do stone masonry really, really well?

Here's a quiz—how many people are described in the Old Testament as "filled with the Spirit of God"? The answer may surprise you. Bezalel is the only one. And let's be honest—he probably wasn't even on your radar screen until you read this passage from Exodus 31! Certainly there are others empowered by the Spirit to do mighty deeds—people like David and Samson—but the only one described as being "filled with the Spirit of God" is Bezalel. And according to this passage, the evidence of Bezalel's Holy Spirit fullness was his ability as a craftsman. The Spirit filled him with this ability to equip him for his work in building the tabernacle.

It is important not to spiritualize our notions of *spiritual gifts* or being *filled with the Spirit*. A spiritual gift is any talent or ability that the Holy Spirit takes hold of and directs to the service of God. And the best definition of what it means to be *filled with the Spirit* is the one Paul himself provides in Colossians 3:16: "Let the message of Christ dwell among you richly." The evidence of that is not limited to our church life or devotional life, but extends also to our work life.

Calvin Seerveld tells this story about his father, a seller of fish at the Great South Bay Fish Market in Long Island, New York:

When I watch my dad's hands, big beefy hands with broad stubby fingers each twice the thickness of mine . . . when I watch those hands delicately split the back of a mackerel or with a swift, true stroke fillet a flounder close to the bone, leaving all the meat together; when I know that these hands dressed and peddled fish from the handlebars of a bicycle in the grim 1930s, cut and sold fish year after year with never a vacation through fire and sickness, thieves and disaster, weariness, winter cold and hot muggy summers, twinkling at work without complaint, past temptations, struggling day in, day out to fix a just price, in weakness often but always in faith consecratedly cutting up fish before the face of the Lord; when I see that, I know God's grace can come down to a man's hand and the flash of a scabby fish knife.

—"In Fulltime Fishmonger Service," *The Banner*, Sept. 3, 1984

I wonder if anyone watched Cal's dad over all those years at the fish market and said, "Now there's a man who is filled with the Spirit!"

I wonder if anyone watching you or me at our daily work would say the same.

Smelly Diapers and the Priesthood of All Believers

"You will be for me a kingdom of priests. . . ."
—*Exodus 19:6*

But you are . . . a royal priesthood. . . .
—*1 Peter 2:9*

I urge you . . . to offer your bodies as a living sacrifice. . . .
—*Romans 12:1*

My wife and I recently basked in the wonder of being first-time grandparents. When our five-month-old granddaughter and her parents lived with us for a month, our home was filled with sights, sounds, and smells we weren't used to experiencing. I especially enjoyed watching my son and his wife "job share" with the diaper-changing duties. "I'll take this one." "My turn!" They took their shifts without complaint, cooing affectionately all through the process.

Isn't "the priesthood of believers" a wonderful thing to behold?

When it comes to our priestly ministry as believers, the first thing we're likely to think of is the glorious truth that we have direct access to God—anytime, anyplace. But there's more. Our priestly ministry also affects the everyday tasks of life, no matter how routine. For it is in carrying out those tasks—at home, at school, at the office or factory—that we offer our selves as living sacrifices. As we carry out our duties, we lift every task to God as an act of priestly worship—even changing smelly diapers!

Consider this quote from Martin Luther's 1522 treatise on "The Estate of Marriage":

> [Natural Reason] . . . turns up her nose and says, "Alas, must I rock the baby, wash its diapers, make its bed, smell its stench, stay up nights with it, take care of it when it cries, heal its rashes and sores, and on top of that care for my wife, provide for her, labour at my trade, take care of this and take care of that, do this and do that, endure this and endure that, and whatever else of bitterness and drudgery married life involves? What, should I make such a prisoner of myself?" . . .
>
> And what does Christian faith say to this? It opens its eyes, looks upon all these insignificant, distasteful and despised duties in the Spirit, and is aware that they are all adorned with divine approval as with the costliest gold and jewels.

What a liberating and affirming perspective on the value of our daily labor, even the most menial and unglamorous tasks! When performed as part of offering ourselves to God, such work—indeed, all work—is an act of worship. It is priestly work, sacred work. It is "holy to the Lord."

A Near Miss

Brothers and sisters, all of you, as responsible to God, should remain in the situation in which God called you.
—*1 Corinthians 7:24*

There are very few movies that I would put on my "must see" or "see it again" list. *Amazing Grace* is one of them. Rent it today if you haven't seen it yet. If you have kids in middle school or above, watch it with them. It's the story of William Wilberforce, one of the greatest, most courageous, yet least known Reformers in the Western world. As a young Member of Parliament in England in the late 1700s, he stood alone in the House of Commons and called for the abolition of the slave trade. It took nearly fifty years before he succeeded.

In his wonderful book *The Call*, Os Guinness tells a side of the story unknown to many:

Perhaps most amazingly of all, William Wilberforce came within a hair's breadth of missing his grand calling altogether. His faith in Jesus Christ animated his lifelong passion for reform. At one stage he led or actively participated in sixty-nine different initiatives, several of world-shaping significance. But when Wilberforce came to faith through the "Great Change" that was his experience of conversion in 1785 at the age of twenty-five, his first reaction was to throw over politics for the ministry. He thought, as millions have thought before and since, that "spiritual" affairs are far more important than "secular" affairs. Fortunately . . . John Newton, the converted slave trader who wrote "Amazing Grace," persuaded Wilberforce that God wanted him to stay in politics rather than enter the ministry. "It's hoped and believed," Newton wrote, "that the Lord has raised you up for the good of the nation." After much prayer and thought, Wilberforce concluded that Newton was right. God was calling him to champion the liberty of the oppressed—as a Parliamentarian.

I wonder how many people become followers of Christ, or experience a revival in their faith along the way, and feel restless to look for a more "spiritual" career path. Perhaps you are one of them. Maybe you wonder if you could serve Christ better or "make a difference for Christ" more significantly if you switched to a job with a Christian organization or ministry.

The Christ-followers in Corinth struggled with such questions two thousand years ago. They wondered if they needed to make wholesale changes in their social situations and commitments now that they had accepted the call to discipleship. Paul's answer was no—God doesn't ask you to stop being Jewish now that you have said yes to Christ's call, as if you can't serve him as a Jew. God doesn't ask you to stop being a Gentile now that you have said yes to Christ's call, as if you can't serve him as a Gentile. And God doesn't ask you to stop being a slave now that you have said yes to Christ's call, as if you can't serve Christ as a slave.

So whether you are a Jew or a Gentile, a slave or a free person is ultimately irrelevant. Whether you are in a dead-end job or find yourself on the fast track in a Fortune 500 company is irrelevant. You don't need to change your circumstances in order to fulfill your highest calling—to serve Christ. Three times within the space of eight verses Paul urges the believers in Corinth "to live as a believer in whatever situation the Lord has assigned to you" (verses 17, 20, 24). In other words, unless you are engaged in work that is clearly contrary to the values and purposes of God's kingdom, stay where you are and serve Christ wholeheartedly right where he has placed you. Let that be your place for ministry.

Just imagine how different the course of history might have been if William Wilberforce had left the situation in which God called him!

Discussion Guide

Opening *(5 minutes)*

Go around the circle and have group members briefly describe their work. Remember that work encompasses more than just a paid job. It can be anything we do to "shape or influence the world around us" as a worker, volunteer, retiree, student, or parent.

Bible Study *(10 minutes)*

Read the following Scripture passages and use the questions to guide your discussion.

- Ephesians 1:15-23
  What do verses 19-23 teach about Jesus Christ? How far does his kingly rule (kingdom) extend?

- Ephesians 6:5-9
  This passage addresses but does not condone or encourage the practice of slavery; rather, Paul offers practical ways of dealing with the realities of the day. For our purposes, read

the passage as applying to the employer/employee situation in general. Given that, what connection do you see between the first passage and the second, with its instructions to slaves?

On the basis of Paul's instructions, do you think he considered the work of slaves to be "kingdom work"? Why or why not? What clues do you find in verses 5-9?

What does all this say about our own work and its importance to God and God's kingdom?

Alternative Approach

In place of the above, read the passages from Matthew 6 cited in question 2 under "Discussion" (on p. 26) and then discuss the question.

Case Study *(10-15 minutes)*

Each discussion guide in this study offers a case study based on actual experiences. If your group decides to use these case studies, you may not have time for all of the "Discussion" questions that follow.

Have someone read the case study below and then discuss the questions that follow.

Emily's Decision

Emily had been offered two new positions—one was managing a new nursing home for the company she already works for; the other was managing a church office. Both jobs sounded great. Today was the day she had to decide.

Maybe the chance to choose between two great jobs sounds good to you—but for Emily it was an agonizing decision.

For ten years she'd worked as a supervisor at a large nursing home. She knew she was good at what she did. The nursing staff respected her as a professional, and even more important, as a friend and mentor. She had a way of being both firm and affirming, and the residents responded well to her. Often she had opportunity to share her faith, and from time to time the residents' family members thanked her warmly for the compassion she showed to their loved ones. Her superiors obviously loved her work or they wouldn't have offered her this promotion at the new home they were opening across town. The new position played to all her strengths, and it would mean more pay and better benefits.

On the other hand, the opportunity to work for the church pulled strongly at Emily's heart. The job as office administrator at a large downtown church would mean less pay and fewer benefits than the new nursing home position, and in some ways she was probably overqualified for the position. But ever since she'd committed her life to Christ in college, Emily had felt a tug toward working in ministry of some kind. As a single mother she couldn't afford to go back to school for a ministry degree. But this would give her the chance to be part of a dynamic staff and be involved in full time "kingdom work." The thought of working in a Christian environment seemed almost too good to be true. What a boost it would be to her faith! And what an honor to be part of a ministry team and make a difference in the lives of so many people!

Emily glanced at the clock. Time was running out. For the umpteenth time she stared at her list of pros and cons. How she wished God would just send her a vision! Better yet, a personal letter! As the deadline approached, she couldn't help but wonder if she were missing something important in her considerations. But what could it be?

If you were a friend of Emily's, what issues would you want to explore with her? What reflection, insight, or Scripture passage from the daily readings might be particularly relevant to these issues?

On the basis of what you know of this case and the issues involved, what would you advise Emily to do? Do a quick survey.

Discussion *(20 minutes)*

1. According to the reading for Day 1, *all* work is ministry. What difference does it (or could it) make to view your daily work as a ministry that God calls you to perform?

2. In Matthew 6 Jesus warns of the distractions that can keep us from seeking first God's kingdom. Storing up treasures on earth is one (verses 19-21). Being consumed by worry is another (verses 25-32). As you think about your own life, what are the things that most distract you from seeking first the kingdom of God in *your* daily work?

3. The reading for Day 3 points out that Bezalel is described as being "filled with the Spirit of God." What difference does it make to you to know that the talents and abilities that you use in your daily work are given to you by the Holy Spirit?

4. According to the reading for Day 4, *all* work is "holy to the Lord"—even changing smelly diapers. What aspects of your own daily work do you have a hard time viewing as sacred? What difference would it make to consciously offer those tasks as part of your daily offering to God?

5. Share one insight from the daily readings you found particularly helpful for the way you view your daily work.

Closing *(5-10 minutes)*

You may want to read this quotation from William Diehl's book *Ministry in Daily Life* as a summary of today's session:

> Many times it has been said that the church should go into the world. The fact is that the church already *is* in the world. It is present in the many Christians who daily labor

in factories and farms, who are faithful husbands and wives, who are caring parents, who uphold society's laws, and who vote on election day. And they minister to others in acts of kindness, by caring for the environment, in love for family, in honesty, and in many other ways. They minister when they are the bearers of hope in a hopeless society.

Have group members share any prayer requests or thanks-givings they may have related to their daily work. Then pray for each other, asking God to give each of you a sense of calling as you serve him and others in your respective workplaces.

Action Options

Choose one of these suggestions for extending the session into the week ahead:

Option 1

Frame each day of your week around the following habits. At the beginning of your day take a couple of minutes to center your thoughts around Jesus' words in Matthew 6:33: "Seek first the kingdom of God and his righteousness." Pray for the Spirit of Christ to guide and empower you in your "kingdom work" for that day. At the end of your day take a few minutes to reflect on what you did that day. As you mentally replay the "video" of your workday, take note of the big or little ways you were able to live out your calling to seek first God's kingdom that day. You may find it encouraging to jot down your thoughts and look them over at the end of the week.

Option 2

Pray this prayer at the start of each workday this week or throughout this study.

> Lord Jesus, as I enter this workplace, I bring your presence with me. I speak your peace, your grace, and your perfect order into this workplace. I acknowledge your lordship over

all that will be spoken, thought, decided, and accomplished here.

Lord Jesus, I thank you for the gifts you have deposited in me. I commit to using them responsibly and well. Give me a fresh supply of truth and beauty to draw on as I do my job. Anoint my creativity, my ideas, my energy so that even my smallest task may bring you honor.

Lord, when I am confused, guide me. When I am weary, energize me. When I am burned out, infuse me with the light of your Holy Spirit. May the work that I do and the way I do it bring hope, life, and courage to all that I come in contact with today.

And even in this day's most stressful moment, may I rest in you. Amen.

Thank God It's Monday!

A Matter of Perspective

So I hated life, because the work that is done under the sun was grievous to me. All of it is meaningless, a chasing after the wind. . . . People can do nothing better than to eat and drink and find satisfaction in their toil. This too, I see, is from the hand of God. . . .
—Ecclesiastes 2:17, 24

About twenty years ago a young man I'll call Brad sat in my office and laid out his plans for the future. He was eighteen at the time, just out of high school. He resolved to go into business for himself and start earning the big bucks. Forget college, he said. By forty he intended to retire, have a place on the lake, and enjoy the good life. Sometimes I wonder if he's on schedule. I picture him driving to work with a bumper sticker on his pickup that says, "I'd rather be fishing."

Everything about Brad's attitude told me he subscribed to the "Thank God It's Friday" philosophy when it comes to daily work. He saw work as a necessary evil—and thus his plan to put it behind him as soon as possible. If Brad's dream doesn't come true, I suspect the words of the Teacher in Ecclesiastes 2:17 will be a fitting description of his sentiments.

Then there's John. He recently turned eighty-five and still goes to work most days at the township treasurer's office. John's philosophy is a little different than Brad's—you might call it "Thank God It's Monday." If it were up to him, the Lord would call him home in the middle of balancing a ledger.

A few years ago John participated in a Bible study I was leading on the book of Ecclesiastes. Before the second lesson was finished I thought he might drop out. He couldn't relate at all to the Teacher's *"Meaningless! Meaningless! Everything is meaningless."* Especially when applied to work! You can imagine his response when our discussion turned to 2:23: "All their days their work is grief and pain; even at night their minds do not rest. This too is meaningless." From the corner of the room John blurted out, "Oh, come on. This is depressing. I love my work!"

John's comment set us up quite nicely to focus on the purpose of Ecclesiastes: "People can do nothing better than to eat and drink and find satisfaction in their toil. This too, I see, is from the hand of God" (verse 24). Note that this refrain is echoed in 3:22: "So I saw that there is nothing better for people than to enjoy their work, because that is their lot."

What a difference your perspective makes! The Teacher understood it well. From one perspective, work is grief and pain and a chasing after the wind. According to Ecclesiastes, this perspective plagues those who see work as simply a means to wealth, pleasure, or fame.

On the other hand, those who truly "find satisfaction in their toil" know that there is "nothing better" for people than to enjoy their work. Such satisfaction and enjoyment is a gift from the hand of God!

How about you? Are you a TGIF person or are you more of a TGIM person? As we'll see in this week's daily readings, "Thank God It's Monday" is a perspective that's deeply rooted in the Creator's design.

"In the Beginning God . . ."

In the beginning God created the heavens and the earth.
—Genesis 1:1

By the seventh day God had finished the
work he had been doing. . . .
—Genesis 2:2

"My Father is always at his work to
this very day, and I too am working."
—John 5:17

love work. OK, *most* days I love work. My wife thinks I might love it too much sometimes. Granted, some days are more taxing than others. Some days I am frustrated because so few items are checked off my "to do" list when I leave the office at the end of the day. And some days are filled with tasks that are more "must do" than "enjoy doing." But usually when the day or week is over, I feel really satisfied. And when a new week begins, I'm much more likely than not to thank God it's Monday.

Maybe I learned that attitude about work from my dad, who modeled for his kids a pretty healthy work ethic. In my earliest memories Dad was a milkman for Garden State Farms Dairy. But for most of my childhood, he was the "Norm" in Johnny & Norm's Drive-In.

Dad put in long hours and late nights. We savored one week of vacation a year because he couldn't take any more time away. When I was old enough to start making fries, I was able to watch Dad closely at the restaurant. Mostly he "found satisfaction in his toil." When a heart condition robbed him of the ability to enjoy a productive retirement, it was painful for him and for the rest of our family.

My father was a worker. From him I learned the value of work. But as disciples, our ultimate model is our Father in heaven.

The very first time we meet God in the Bible, in the very first verse of Genesis, he is working: "In the beginning God created the heavens and the earth." And by the second chapter in the creation story, we've discovered that God put in a full six-day week. "By the seventh day God finished the work he had been doing" (Genesis 2:2). Which doesn't mean God's work was finished, period. It means, as we'll explore further in our next reading, that everything was in place for his image-bearing partners—that's you and me—to assume the role of managing and developing the world God created.

But even with his human partners in place, God is still a worker. In the language of theology, God's work of creation is intimately related to his work of providence—that is, his ongoing work of preserving and governing the universe God called into being. Read Psalm 104 for a wonderful rehearsal and celebration of God's daily work of providing for his myriad creatures.

When sin enters the picture in Genesis 3, God's work of salvation kicks into full gear, causing the psalmist to declare, "Great are the works of the LORD; they are pondered by all who delight in them" (Psalm 111:2). As Jesus acknowledged, both he and his Father never stop being workers: "My Father is always at his work to this very day, and I too am working" (John 5:17).

Nowhere in the pages of Scripture do we hear God complaining about going to work. He may complain that his human creatures resist his work or fail to honor him for his work. But God doesn't complain about going to work. It is God's nature to be a worker. As his followers, we can learn from this truth. If we truly want to allow our attitude about work to be shaped by God's Word, then we should heed the advice of the psalmist and devote ourselves to "pondering" the works of the Lord. The more we do, the more likely we'll be to thank God for Monday mornings.

DAY 3

Mirrors in the Marketplace

Then God said, "Let us make human beings in our image, in our likeness, so that they may rule over the fish . . . and the birds . . . , over the livestock and all the wild animals, and all the creatures that move along the ground." So God created human beings in his own image. . . . God blessed them and said to them, "Be fruitful and increase in number; fill the earth and subdue it. Rule over the fish . . . and the birds . . . and over every living creature. . . ."
—Genesis 1:26-28

One September Sunday in 2007 my wife, Annelies, and I got to hear our youngest child preach for the very first time. There he stood in the pulpit I had occupied for fifteen years. It was a wonderful experience, perhaps more nerve-wracking for us than for him. Afterward we were the recipients of many gracious comments from the congregation: "It was like listening to a younger version of Ken—same mannerisms, same dry sense of humor. . . . A chip off the old block!"

It's amazing and sometimes scary to discover how much our looks, mannerisms, habits, and other personality traits are

36

mirrored in our children. It's almost as if husbands and wives everywhere had resolved together, "Let us make a human being in our image, in our likeness. . . ."

That, of course, is what the triune God resolved to do before the sixth day of creating was over. Everything else was in place. All the other creatures had been called into being when God decided to fashion a creature who would bear his image. God made human beings.

"The image of God" is an important doctrine in Christian teaching. Where and how we reflect God has been the subject of much discussion and debate in the church through the centuries. Some point to our human capacity to reason, our intelligence, our moral character, and our creativity as godlike qualities.

But the godlike character that stands out most in Genesis 1 is our calling as workers! As we saw in yesterday's reading, it is the very nature of God to be a worker. So it shouldn't surprise us that one of the primary ways we reflect God's image is in our own work.

According to the command and blessing of God in Genesis 1:26-28, God calls us to rule (how godlike is that?!), to fill, to subdue. In *Engaging God's World*, Cornelius Plantinga Jr. comments on what this means for our task in the world:

> To image God, then, human beings are charged not only with care for earth and animals ("subduing" what's already there) but also with developing certain cultural possibilities ("filling" out what is only potentially there). To unfold such possibilities—for example, to speak languages, build tools and dies, enter contracts, organize dance troupes—is to act in character for human beings designed by God. That is, to act in this way is to exhibit some of God's own creativity and dominion in a characteristically human way.

What a wonderfully affirming perspective this gives us for our daily work! Every day that you and I spend at work, we are God's mirrors in the marketplace. In the work that we do and in the way we do it, we provide a visible picture of an invisible God for those around us.

Which gives us yet another reason to say, "Thank God it's Monday"!

The First (and Best) Partnership

*The LORD God took the man and put him in the
Garden of Eden to work it and take care of it.*

—*Genesis 2:15*

'␣ve already told you about Johnny & Norm's Drive-In.
Norm was my dad and Johnny was his partner. As far as
business partnerships go, theirs was a good one. I realize
that Johnny & Norm's was small potatoes (actually French
Fries) in the business community, but Dad and Johnny enjoyed
some wonderful years together. They trusted each other, were
committed to each other, and shared the same values in running
the business.

Whether we're talking Johnny & Norm's or AOL and
TimeWarner, partnerships in the marketplace are risky. When
they click, they're great. They provide security and the pleasure
of shared resources and accomplishments. But when the
partners are not in sync they can be awful.

The best and most productive partnership of all is the first one
ever forged, described in Genesis 2:15: God planted a garden.

Then he partnered with Adam (and his family) to manage the day-to-day operations. "The LORD God took the man and put him in the Garden of Eden to work it and take care of it" ("till it and keep it," RSV).

In this partnership we humans are assigned a double task. The first is to "work" ("till") the garden. One translation uses the word *cultivate*. Notice how closely this word is linked to the word *culture*. When we speak of "North American culture" we are talking about the particular ways in which people in this part of the world think and act together. Culture has to do with so many areas of our life together—economics, business, politics, entertainment, education, family life, music and the arts, and so on. In all of these there is something distinctive about Canadian or American culture that is quite different from the culture of Bolivia or Nigeria or Indonesia.

Now you can see why theologians speak of a "cultural mandate" in Genesis 1. As partners, God entrusts us with the task of cultivating, of unfolding culture in ways that honor him and are true to his laws. The workplace is one area where we fulfill this task. Every workplace has its own culture, reflected in the values, priorities, and ways people relate—employers and employees, clients and customers, coworkers. God asks us to use our influence to help shape that culture in ways that reflect the values of God's kingdom. Ordinarily, employers and managers have greater influence than others, but each of us has *some* influence. It's all part of our task of "working" or cultivating God's garden!

Our second task in this partnership is that of "keeping" the garden. God asks us to take care of, or preserve, the garden. The word for "keep" is the same one found in the familiar Aaronic blessing in Numbers 6:24: "The LORD bless you and keep you." Just as the Lord "keeps" us—that is, protects and cares for us— we are to protect and care for all that God has entrusted to us. We do not have license to exploit God's good creation; instead our job is to exercise stewardship over it. "The earth is the LORD's, and everything in it" says the psalmist in Psalm 24:1. In the words of the contemporary testimony *Our World Belongs to God*, we are "appointed earth keepers and caretakers to tend the earth, enjoy it, and love our neighbors. God uses our skills for the unfolding and well-being of his world" (paragraph 10).

You and I have the remarkable privilege of being partners with God in the ongoing work of cultivating and caring for God's creation! When the psalmist contemplated the significance of this partnership, he broke into song: "What are mere mortals that you are mindful of them, human beings that you care for them? You have made them a little lower than the heavenly beings and crowned them with glory and honor. You made them rulers over the works of your hands; you put everything under their feet" (Psalm 8:4-6).

And as we contemplate the dignity God has conferred on our work, we find yet another reason to say "Thank God it's Monday!"

Work IS Worship

*"'Love the Lord your God with all your heart and with
all your soul and with all your mind and with all
your strength.' . . . 'Love your neighbor as yourself.'
There is no commandment greater than these."*

—Mark 12:30-31

What's the first thing that comes to mind when you hear the word *worship*?

For most of us, it's probably something related to what we do on Sundays. We might say something like, "Our worship is awesome!" or "Our church is really into 'blended worship,' how about yours?"

The Westminster Shorter Catechism affirms a core biblical truth: "The chief purpose of human beings" is "to glorify God and enjoy him forever." In other words, our chief purpose is worship! In our church, we love to sing this beautiful song: "In our lives, Lord, be glorified, be glorified." We add stanzas depending on the occasion—"In our homes, Lord . . ."; "in our schools, Lord . . ."; "in your world, Lord . . ." The lyrics remind us that worship—glorifying God—is not just something we do on Sunday. It's something we express every day, everywhere, in all that we do—even in our work.

In the opening chapters of the Bible we discover God's design for creation, including you and me. What is our primary task as God's image-bearers? What is the worshipful response God calls us to offer? It's *work*. Our chief purpose is to rule, to fill, to subdue, to cultivate and care for the garden. Work!

That means we can't separate our work from our worship. Work is worship. Before there was such as thing as a "worship service," there was the worshipful service of human work in partnership with God.

Jesus' familiar words in today's Scripture passage shed light on how we are to express our worship in our daily work. Jesus' call to love God above all and our neighbor as ourselves is a response to the law-teacher's question about which of the commandments is most important. As God often reminds his Old Testament people, the worship that he desires most is not formal ritual. It is the worship of obedience. To obey the law of love, the greatest of God's commandments, is the worship that glorifies God best. Such worship cannot be contained in an hour or two in the sanctuary on Sunday.

Consider the opportunities you have every day in your work to express the love of Christ to your neighbor. Whether you're an at-home parent caring for your preschooler, a cashier at the grocery store, a painter, an administrative assistant in a large office, or a business owner—whatever you do—you are providing goods and services that make life better for others. Your income provides food, shelter, and clothing for the "neighbors" who are your own family *and* for yourself. Your work also gives you the opportunity to show generosity to those in need.

Through our daily work we show love for God—through the commitments we express (heart), the emotions we exhibit (soul), the way we use our intellect (mind), and the energy we expend (strength). "Whatever you do, work at it with all your heart, *as working for the Lord*," writes Paul to the Colossian Christians, "not for human masters [or employers], since you know that you will receive an inheritance from the Lord as a reward. It is the Lord Christ you are serving" (Colossians 3:23-24).

Going about our work day by day in ways that express love for our neighbors and for our God is truly worshipful work. Still another reason why we can say, "Thank God it's Monday!"

Discussion Guide

Opening *(5-10 minutes)*

Give each person in the group an opportunity to share an insight or learning from the daily readings that was particularly helpful. At this point just listen to the comments without evaluation or discussion.

Bible Study *(15 minutes)*

Read the following Scripture passages and use the questions to guide your study. If you wish, divide the passages among smaller groups and report back to the larger group.

• Genesis 2:15-17

What specific command did God give Adam?

What specific limitation did God impose on Adam?

Why is it important for us in our daily work to experience both freedom *and* responsibility?

- Ecclesiastes 2:17-26

  What do you think the Teacher observed about work (and workers) that led him to the dismal view of work that dominates this passage (verses 17-23)?

  What do you think the Teacher observed about work (and workers) that led him to the positive view of work that emerges in verses 24-25?

Case Study *(10 minutes)*

Each discussion guide in this study offers a case study that is based on true experiences. If you decide to use these case studies, you may not have time to use all of the "Discussion" questions that follow.

Read aloud the case study below, then discuss the questions that follow it.

Dream Job

From: "Travis Miller" <travmill@yahoo.com>
To: <popmiller@hotmail.com>
Date: Fri, 06 Jun 2009 18:23:54
Subject: Dream Job!

Hey Dad!

How's it going? Here's a quick update on what's happening in Denver. It's been another long week—over 60 hours. (Good thing I'm not married yet, right?!) But this is a dream job! This city has everything—friendly people, great food, good theater, sports that won't quit, churches (I'm still looking). And it doesn't take long to get out into the mountains to go backpacking. When you and Mom come out, I'll show you all the sights.

The people in the office have gone out of their way to make me feel at home. My boss can be kind of a jerk, but he's had me out to his condo in the mountains a couple of times already for parties. And he's obviously happy with my work—it's been, what, three months?—and already he's given me a raise!

So even if sitting at a desk all day isn't exactly my idea of a good time, I'm feeling pretty good about this job. In a way, I miss sales—it was always pressure, but I was pretty good at it. Can't have everything though. This job is better pay and the perks are a huge plus. So I think it was a good move.

Give my love to Mom. I'll call this weekend.

Travis

In answering the following questions, you may want to draw on the reading for Day 2.

What is it about Travis's job that makes it a "dream job"?

If you were Travis's parent or friend, how might this e-mail convince you (or not) that he has truly found his "dream job"?

On the basis of this e-mail, what is Travis's underlying perspective on life and work?

Discussion (20 minutes)

1. How would you describe *your* perspective on your daily work? Are you a "Thank God It's Friday" person or a "Thank God It's Monday" person? Or are you somewhere in between? What influences play the greatest role in shaping your perspective? Go around the circle and give each person opportunity to respond.

2. The reading for Day 3 says that every day at work we are "God's mirrors in the marketplace," giving those around us a visible picture of an invisible God. Think of some opportunities you have to "mirror God" in your daily work.

3. Share some opportunities you have to influence ("cultivate") the culture of your workplace in the direction of God's design (Day 4).

4. These days, much attention is given to environmental concerns—for example, global warming, clean water, and efficient use of energy. How does God's command to take care of ("keep") the garden influence your involvement in environmental issues?

5. Do you believe that your daily work is worship? What makes it that way?

Alternative Approach

Instead of using the questions above, try the following (or discuss an issue from the readings that concerns the group):

- On one sheet of newsprint list all the reasons you can think of collectively for being able to say "Thank God it's Monday"!

- On another sheet list all the reasons why you are inclined (at least some weeks) to say "Thank God it's Friday!"

What advice would you give to fellow group members or others who feel that their workplace culture is strongly resistant or even hostile to a "kingdom" influence?

If your group is large, you may want to form smaller groups of three to five each to work on the activity. Afterward display the lists and present them to the large group.

Closing *(5 minutes)*

You may want to summarize today's session by reading the following:

> As a human created in God's image, you are inherently significant, and when you work you are doing something that is very godlike. It is not only God's work that is significant; human work is significant, too. It is something ordained by God. The fact that you work is, in the words of Genesis 1, "very good." Intrinsically good. Valued by God.
>
> —Doug Sherman and William Hendricks,
> *Your Work Matters to God*

Close by sharing any prayer requests or thanksgivings related to your daily work. In particular, share any workplace frustrations that stand in the way of finding satisfaction in your work. Bring these before God in prayer, asking especially for God to lead the way for each person to experience greater fulfillment in serving God and others in their daily work.

Action Options

Choose one of the following suggestions for extending the session into the week ahead:

Option 1

Think about your work as a potential blessing of God. Take a few minutes to jot down at least three goals that you could bring to your daily work as a result. Write them down on a note card and carry it with you for the rest of this week.

Option 2

Rewrite Psalm 8:5-9 using the first person singular: "You have made me a little lower than the heavenly beings and crowned me with glory and honor . . ." For the next week, begin and end each day by reading these verses as a prayer of praise. Consider memorizing the verses so you can hold them in your heart throughout the day. Ask God to use them to inspire you with your high calling as God's coworker.

Option 3

Recite, hum, or sing in your heart the words from the song "Be Glorified." "In my work, Lord, be glorified. Be glorified. In my work, Lord, be glorified today." Carry these words with you throughout your next work day. Include them with your morning prayer. Pray them as you go to work and during breaks throughout the day. At the end of the day, meditate on the ways you were able to glorify God in your work that day.

Take This Job and Shove It!

Labor Pains

"Cursed is the ground because of you; through painful toil you will eat of it all the days of your life. It will produce thorns and thistles for you. . . . By the sweat of your brow you will eat your food. . . ."
—*Genesis 3:17-19*

We know that the whole creation has been groaning as in the pains of childbirth right up to the present time.
—*Romans 8:22*

My first paid job was delivering *The Paterson Evening News* in our neighborhood in Wyckoff, New Jersey. As a youngster I was excited about this new venture. I had a "real" job. I would actually make money! Of course there were responsibilities—delivering the papers on time every day, keeping straight who was on vacation, and collecting the money. I felt like a big shot and dove in with determination.

As I recall, the luster didn't last long. I discovered that even neighbors could be mean and disagreeable. So could their dogs. Getting some people to pay on time was impossible. Delivering papers in the rain was miserable. Delivering papers in the sunshine when my friends were playing baseball was even more miserable. Some people didn't smile much. Some people complained a lot. And yes, sometimes I would miss houses or forget who was on vacation.

It didn't take me long to have second thoughts about how great working is or to reach the conclusion that earning money isn't all it's cracked up to be. Call it a reality check for a ten-year-old.

Hardly a day goes by without "reality checks" in the workaday world. A disgruntled worker marches into an office complex with an automatic weapon and guns down coworkers. A company official engages in fraudulent practices. An employee brings allegations of sexual harassment against her boss. Labor negotiations break down. Most people don't have to look very far to find instances of corporate greed, unsafe work conditions, managerial favoritism, unfair competition, unreasonable demands, inadequate wages, unethical accounting practices, workers taking advantage of their bosses, racial discrimination, workplace monotony, or morally unhealthy office environments.

Contrast these "realities" with God's calling to honor him and bless our neighbors by serving and loving them in our work; to find fulfillment and blessing in caring for creation; to worship God in our work.

It comes as no surprise that the realities of the marketplace do not measure up to God's design. As the biblical story tells us, our first parents disobeyed God and sin entered the picture. Because of sin, all of life suffers. We fail to honor God in our daily work. We fail to unfold the creation for his glory. Our relationship with our neighbors at work is often characterized by envy, deception, and selfishness instead of love. We find ourselves frustrated in our daily work instead of fulfilled. Our personal motives are often tainted. And instead of caring for and blessing God's creation, we abuse it for our own gain.

As a result of sin's curse, the very environment we are called to "work and care for" (Genesis 2:15) resists our efforts. Agriculture is more difficult. Harnessing energy is enormously challenging and costly. Our daily work may be physically and emotionally draining. Some days and weeks it truly feels like we complete our tasks "by the sweat of our brow."

The whole creation, Paul says, was "subjected to frustration" through the disobedience of our first parents. "The whole creation has been groaning as in the pains of childbirth right up to the present time." In other words, sin's distortion is everywhere. There's not a workplace anywhere in the world, including yours or mine, where that frustration is not felt and that groaning is not heard.

Working in Babylon

Then the king [Nebuchadnezzar] ordered Ashpenaz, chief of his court officials, to bring into the king's service some of the Israelites from the royal family and the nobility. . . . He was to teach them the language and literature of the Babylonians. . . . They were to be trained for three years, and after they were to enter the king's service.
—*Daniel 1:3-5*

I t was the summer of '72. I was in Wildwood, New Jersey, together with about ten other college students. Our primary reason for spending the summer in this seaside resort was evangelism—to volunteer our time working with the Boardwalk Chapel. Every evening we handed out tracts, shared the gospel with passersby, and sang gospel music.

During the day we worked for a food distributing company. Nothing I had experienced before while working in my father's restaurant or attending college quite prepared me for this. The language was vulgar, the warehouse manager had an attitude about "religious" people, and centerfolds adorned the walls of the bathroom. Everything about the environment seemed like an assault on my faith.

Imagine the contrast: days at "Babylon Warehouse," evenings at Boardwalk Chapel!

Maybe you feel the same contrast each week when you move from Sunday to Monday, from a day of worship and spiritual renewal to a workplace or classroom where your faith is on trial every day. Maybe you work in a place where your Christian values are openly or subtly ridiculed or marginalized. Or maybe your workplace culture is polite and respectful but the corporate or office or shop floor values are so thoroughly at odds with the values of your faith that you feel an awkward "disconnect" between your home and church and your workplace environment. Maybe you feel the pressure to conform every single day in your workplace.

Daniel and his companions faced that pressure in the courts of Nebuchadnezzar. To survive and flourish in "the king's service" they were expected to conform to the ways of Babylon—its values, its language, its culture, even its food. It was all part of a reprogramming initiative, what we might call "Babylonization." For their own good Daniel and his fellow exiles were pressured to forsake their Israelite ways and give in.

Of course your employer or manager or CEO or principal is not Nebuchadnezzar. But you may still feel pressure at work—pressure to behave certain ways, to embrace certain values, to adopt certain priorities, to speak a certain language. Pressure to get along, fit in. The unspoken message is, If you would just conform, you would be happy.

In our setting this "re-programming" effort is called secularization. It reminds us how deep the impact of sin is on the world of work. It's not just about me or my relationships or what someone else is doing to me in the workplace. It's much bigger and deeper than that. The system itself is distorted by the effects of sin.

So every day when we show up at work, we face an integrity check, just as Daniel and his companions did. Every day we get to make a choice: to conform or to resist.

What will you choose?

Idolatry

"You shall have no other gods before me."
—Exodus 20:3

"No one can serve two masters. Either you will hate the one and love the other, or you will be devoted to the one and despise the other. You cannot serve both God and Money."
—Matthew 6:24

Bonnie was exceptionally bright—near the top of her class all the way through school. She grew up in a Christian home with hard-working parents who taught her well and who modeled for her what it means to follow Jesus. After high school she went on to a Christian college where she maintained a 4.0 grade point average and earned a pre-architecture degree. After college she headed to grad school, and from there she launched into the marketplace. Bonnie showed all the signs of embracing a Christian worldview. She was full of sound principles, a drive to succeed, and a sense of calling to make a difference in the world.

That was fifteen years ago. In terms of our culture's standards of success, Bonnie has done very well. She's a partner in a reputable firm—a poster child for "small-town girl makes big." She owns a beautiful condo in the city and a cottage on the lake for weekends way.

In terms of living out her calling, Bonnie was not doing so well the last time I connected with her. She admitted that her connection to God was tenuous at best, and her connection to the church was practically severed. She no longer felt a sense of calling to make a difference in God's kingdom.

Bonnie's story illustrates the truth of Jesus' warning "You cannot serve both God and Money."

Many "gods" tempt us to place them before the true God. Many masters call us to serve them instead of or alongside of God. From the perspective of her peers and admirers, Bonnie became a great success. From the perspective of God's Word, Bonnie became an "idolater"—that is, she began to trust in something instead of or alongside of God (see Heidelberg Catechism, Q&A 95).

All of us face the temptation of idolatry in the workplace. It might be the temptation to sell our souls to the god of money, status, or career. But it might also be that for us the stronger temptation is to divide our allegiance—to divide our lives into two parts, devoting Sunday to the Lord and the rest of the week to ourselves and our pursuit of profit or career.

In her study of over eighty-five Christian CEOs and top executives, Laura Nash discovered that many of them take precisely this approach to life. "Business is business, religion is religion. . . . There are the Sunday rules and values and there are the workplace rules and values, and never the twain shall meet" (*Believers in Business*). But such a division of life and loyalties is impossible because you *cannot* (notice Jesus doesn't say *should not*) serve both God and money.

No one can force us choose idolatry. Although the temptation is there, you and I do not have to yield. In our last reading we saw that sin is systemic. It shapes the patterns and values and priorities that permeate the workplace, it pressures us to conform. But sin is also deeply personal. It is evident in the choices that you and I make every day.

In other words, it's not just the workplace that is affected and distorted by sin. It's the workers. It's you and me. I can say all I want about evil in the workplace. But if I choose to put money or success or career before God, or if I try to give God my Sundays and home life but devote my daily work to career advancement or wealth building above serving my neighbor, then I am guilty of idolatry. I have chosen to serve something other than God in my daily work.

So whether you're just launching your career, or moving up the ladder, or growing weary in the search for a job—any job, take to heart these closing words of 1 John: "Dear children, keep yourselves from idols."

Temptation in the Workplace

*Now Joseph was well-built and handsome, and after a while his
master's wife took notice of Joseph and said, "Come to bed with me!"*
—*Genesis 39:6-7*

D oris was a waitress at my father's restaurant. She got
along great with customers. She was dependable, a hard
worker, and she rarely missed a shift. She was one of
Dad's favorites. Then one day a long-time regular called dad
over. "Norm, I hate to tell you this, but Doris is stealing from
you. I've been watching her over the last couple of weeks. She's
pocketing some of the money that should go into the till."

Dad could hardly believe it. But it only took a day of careful
watching to see the painful truth in front of him. He was
devastated.

There's not a job in the world that is free from temptation.
It doesn't matter if you work in a store, a school, a factory, an
office, or a church. Opportunities for sin abound. Maybe you're
a bookkeeper who realizes just how easy it would be to fudge the
numbers and skim some cash off the top for yourself. Or maybe

you've noticed that sexual favors or flirtatious behavior will move you up the corporate ladder much faster than diligence and integrity. Or you sit in a cubicle knowing you could waste hours of company time every day playing games on your computer and no one will figure it out. Or in my own work, you find that it's a lot easier to download sermons from the web than write your own—*and the congregation would probably like them better!*

Temptation. It's yet another reality of the work environment that reveals the effects of sin. Instead of the workplace being a setting for joyful and worshipful service to God, sin has turned it into a spiritual battleground. Temptation is one of the devil's prime tools for luring us into compromising behavior.

But consider what it does to our Christian witness when we yield to temptation. The story of Joseph being tempted by Potiphar's wife illustrates what's at stake. It would have been so easy for Joseph to compromise himself! We know from the book of Genesis that God had big plans for using Joseph as an instrument to accomplish his saving plans. Satan knew the damage it would do to God's work in the world if he could only lure Joseph into abandoning his integrity and allegiance to God.

The same thing is at stake for us when we face temptation in the workplace. In Week 1 of this study we talked about how we are called to kingdom work regardless of what kind of job we have. We are called to "seek first God's kingdom and his righteousness" in whatever work environment we find ourselves.

Maybe we don't think we'll ever measure up to Joseph when it comes to making a difference in God's kingdom. But the truth is, we might never see or understand the impact we have in our workplaces when we continue to act with integrity and stay true to God's kingdom values. What we do know is this: it is a great victory for Satan if we yield to temptation and compromise ourselves at work.

"Am I My Brother's Keeper?"

Then the LORD said to Cain, "Where is your brother Abel?"
"I don't know," he replied. "Am I my brother's keeper?"
—Genesis 4:9

Mike enjoyed his job at the warehouse. The pay wasn't so hot, but it was steady work and at least the job came with modest benefits. He was hard-working and dependable. His supervisor, George, noticed and appreciated Mike's good work. That led to some overtime opportunities, which helped Mike earn a little extra to help pay his wife's medical bills. Mike's wife struggled with a chronic medical condition.

George cared about Mike's family circumstances. He regularly asked Mike how things were going at home, and he willingly adjusted Mike's schedule from time to time so he could take his wife to her doctor appointments. If an occasional emergency at home caused him to be a bit late, George would cut him some slack and allow him to make it up at the end of the day.

Then George was moved to another plant. From the first time Mike met Karen, the new supervisor, he sensed that things were going to be different. She told him that his hours were set, that she expected him to be at work on time, and that if he needed to take personal time he would have to request it. Mike told Karen about the situation at home but that didn't sway her a bit. "We all have something," she said. "Obviously I can't start adjusting for you, or else I'll have to do it with everybody." Karen never asked Mike about how his wife was doing. She was "all business." Over the next six months she wrote Mike up four times for being late and gave him an unfavorable performance review. He appealed, but that only served to heighten his sense that Karen was on his case. A few months later, Mike was out of a job.

This week we are looking at the various ways sin affects the workplace. We've seen how it can distort the whole workplace environment—the values, priorities, habits, and expectations—that pressure us to conform and accept "the way things are." We've also seen how sin can affect us personally, tempting us to make gods out of our work or careers or earnings. Mike's story illustrates still another effect of sin in the workplace. It damages *relationships*.

Sin tempts us to give in to impulses of envy, jealousy, pride, or vindictiveness in our work instead of embracing our workplaces as opportunities to love and serve our neighbors. Clearly Mike's experience is not isolated. The United States Equal Employment Opportunity Commission reports a 125-percent-increase in racial discrimination charges since the mid-1990s. The Commission also notes an increase in age and gender discrimination in the workplace. Discrimination, favoritism, harassment, gossip, hostile office environments, and unfair wages are among the evils that plague so many workplaces—and all are evidence of the effect of sin on human relationships.

As you read this, you may be thinking of your own unpleasant or distressing experiences with workplace relationships. Maybe you finally left a job because the social environment was so unhealthy, or you've paid the price for a manager's favoritism or a coworker's bullying. Or maybe you've made life miserable for a coworker or someone you supervise.

After Cain attacked and killed his brother, Abel, the Lord came to him and asked where Abel was. Cain replied, "I don't know. Am I my brother's keeper?" Cain's response shows just how deeply sin had gripped his heart and how far removed his attitude was from what God intended. If he were still in tune with God's design for life and work, he never would have asked that question.

The answer, of course, is yes. *Yes,* you are your brother's keeper. God's wants us to love and care for one another.

If God were to ask today for a report on the welfare of your fellow workers, customers, or employees, would you respond with the sinful question Cain asked so long ago—Am I my brother's keeper? Am I my sister's keeper?

Instead, let's use our opportunities in the workplace to cultivate relationships and look out for one another—and in so doing fulfill our calling to glorify God and bless our neighbors.

Discussion Guide

Opening *(5-10 minutes)*

Choose one of the following options to open your session.

Option 1

The theme for this week is the effect of sin on the world of work. Try to keep some balance in today's group discussion by taking turns sharing one encouraging or positive thing that you experienced in your work in the past week. Remember that work encompasses more than a person's occupation—it is anything we do to "shape and influence the world around us, including other people" at home, in the community, or in paid employment.

Option 2

A recent survey shows that only 45 percent of Americans are happy with their work—the lowest level of satisfaction in more than twenty-two years of studying the issue. Do you find this attitude reflected in some of the people you work with? Among your friends or acquaintances? What do you think accounts for it?

Bible Study *(15 minutes)*

Read the following Scripture passage and use the questions to guide your discussion.

- Genesis 3:6-13

  What effect did the fall into sin have on Adam and Eve as individuals? In other words, what personal behaviors or attitudes did they exhibit *after* they sinned that they did not exhibit *before*? How or where do you see such behaviors and attitudes in your own work environment?

  What effect did the fall into sin have on Adam and Eve's relationship with each other? How or where do you see the effects of sin on relationships in today's work environment? How about in your own work environment or workplace relationships?

  What effect did the fall into sin have on Adam and Eve's relationship with God? How or where do you see the effect of sin on people's relationship with God in your own work environment?

Case Study *(15 minutes)*

Have someone read the case aloud, then discuss the questions that follow it. You may want to draw on the reading for Day 3 when discussing the questions. Remember that discussing the case study means you may not have time for all of the "Discussion" questions.

On Days Like This I Hate My Job!

"How in the world did I get into this mess?" Rachelle wondered.

At the suggestion of an employee who reported to her, Rachelle had hired Lucy to do secretarial work on a part-time basis. Lucy was a family friend of the employee who recommended her.

In truth, the need for her services was questionable. But when Rachelle heard of Lucy's challenging family circumstances, she decided to make the hire. It may not have been the best management decision from a financial perspective, but Rachelle knew she had the latitude to do it. Lucy needed a break, and it seemed like the Christian thing to do.

After a fairly positive start, a few months into the job Lucy's performance and behavior became problematic. Others in the office complained that she was moody and unpredictable. Morale was deteriorating, and the quality of Lucy's work was slipping. She simply wasn't performing up to expectations.

When Rachelle scheduled a meeting to address her concerns, Lucy confided that that she had been diagnosed with bipolar disorder, and that keeping the job was critical to her return to normal functioning. With Lucy's permission, Rachelle discussed the situation with Lucy's psychologist as well as with the staff psychologist. Both agreed that a setback in this job could trigger a significant and possibly permanent psychological spiral.

Rachelle truly wanted Lucy to succeed. But she also had an obligation to the rest of the staff. Meanwhile, she was responsible for performance and production in her department. Although she felt sorry for Lucy, compassion in this case was not likely to score points with her superiors.

Something had to be done, and soon. Rachelle was leaving for business trip in a couple of days, and she didn't want to leave this situation unresolved. Taking a deep breath, she reviewed her options one more time. She could simply fire Lucy for substandard performance. She could try to transfer for her to another position within the company. One thing was painfully clear. There was no way to avoid terminating Lucy in her current position.

Rachelle sighed. "Why can't I find a 'win-win' solution to this one? On days like this I hate my job!"

Identify the elements of this case that indicate that we live in a fallen world.

What Bible passages or Christian teachings relate to these issues?

On the basis of what you know of this case and the issues involved, what do you think Rachelle should do?

Alternative Approach
Divide into small groups of two to five persons each. Ask each group to decide what Rachelle should do and why, and then share their findings with the large group.

Discussion *(20 minutes)*

1. Share one or two of the most frustrating aspects of your daily work. Is it mainly the work itself, the work environment, or something in you as a worker?

2. The reading for Day 2 describes Daniel's experience working for Nebuchadnezzar in Babylon. In terms of your daily work, how well can you relate to his experience? When, if ever, in your work experience have you felt pressured to behave in ways that are inconsistent with your Christian values?

3. Work has become an idol for many people in our culture. How do you know when work is your idol? (See Day 3.)

4. "Maybe we don't think we'll ever measure up to Joseph when it comes to making a difference in God's kingdom. But the truth is, we might never see or understand the impact we have in our workplaces when we continue to act with integrity and stay true to God's kingdom values" (Day 4). Describe a time when you—or a fellow employee—made an impact in the workplace by acting with integrity and staying true to God's values.

5. How or where do you find encouragement and strength to face or overcome the effects of sin in your daily work?

Closing *(5 minutes)*

You may want to read this summary statement of the week's readings:

> Sin affects the workplace by distorting the whole workplace environment—values, priorities, habits, and expectations—and pressuring us to conform and accept "the way things are." Sin also affects us personally, tempting us to make gods out of our work or careers or earnings. And sin can damage relationships in the workplace.

Take a couple of minutes of silence to think about a relationship in your work setting that you find particularly challenging. During the silence, you may confess your struggle to God in prayer and ask for the Holy Spirit to empower you with a more Christlike attitude and behavior toward this person.

Close by praying the words of Psalm 51:10-12 together:

"Create in me a pure heart, O God, and renew a steadfast spirit within me. Do not cast me from your presence or take your Holy Spirit from me. Restore to me the joy of your salvation and grant me a willing spirit, to sustain me."

Action Options

Choose one of the following suggestions for extending the session into the week ahead:

Option 1

In light of this week's theme, include a time for daily confession in your daily devotions. Each day in the coming week, devote some time to confessing before God your struggle with sin in your daily work. Ask for God's forgiveness and grace as you address your struggles in your workplace. You may also want to say Psalm 51:10-12 (above) as part of your prayer.

Option 2

Take a few moments to begin composing a brief mission statement for your daily work. Make it a statement that expresses your commitment and desire to keep God *first* in your daily work. (Since writing such statements usually takes careful reflection and several drafts, think of this as a preliminary draft, the first step in the process. In the weeks to come you may choose to spend more time on it.)

Improved Conditions

Redemption Reaches the Workplace

He who was seated on the throne said,
"I am making everything new!"

—Revelation 21:5

ost Christians have some understanding about the biblical concepts of *sin* and *salvation*. Last week we explored the disastrous effects of the fall into sin. We saw how the effects of sin reach into the world of work and even into our own life and attitudes and behavior as workers. That's sin.

Christians generally agree that salvation comes through the death and resurrection of Jesus. But they don't all agree about what that means for the workplace.

For example, some Christians think of salvation in terms of confessing Jesus as their "personal Lord and Savior." That might mean that Jesus forgives their sins. Or that they receive the gift of eternal life. But does it have anything to do with their daily work? Is salvation simply something that enables Christians to look beyond the drudgery and disappointments of this life—

and our work—to a joyful future in heaven? Does confessing Jesus as our personal Lord and Savior have any impact on the way we work or on our workplace?

It's clear that salvation means transformed hearts and lives. But does the transforming power of Jesus Christ extend beyond our personal hearts and lives into the world around us—into society, culture, and the *workplace*?

The gospel's answer to that question is a resounding and joyful *yes*. The transforming power of salvation through Jesus Christ is just as deep and extensive as the transforming power of sin. Sin affects the whole creation. Redemption embraces the whole creation. Human sin causes all the misery. Christ died and rose again to atone for that sin. Wherever sin has made a mess of God's good creation, Christ comes with power to redeem and restore.

The salvation we have in Christ is all-embracing. Jesus saves not just our souls but our whole life, even our physical existence. As Christians we believe in "the resurrection of the body." So redemption does not mean being rescued *out of* the created world in order to be catapulted into heaven. Instead it means that in Christ, God is making "everything new."

This has enormous implications for our daily work. Even our work and workplaces are touched and reshaped by the power of Christ's saving work.

And it begins with you and me. When the power of Christ's salvation takes hold of our hearts and lives, *we* are transformed. Our attitudes, our motivations, our behaviors are all changed and redirected. Instead of making idols of our careers or our paychecks or our businesses, we devote them to God as a means to serve him and others.

Instead of being intimidated by the "principalities and powers" (Ephesians 6, KJV) that influence the marketplace, we are able by the power of the Holy Spirit to stand up in Christ's name and resist. We are able to submit to the influence of his Word and the values of his kingdom.

Instead of using our workplace skills and opportunities for personal advantage and exploiting the environment for the sake of our lifestyles and comfort, we rediscover the joyful calling to be stewards of all that God has entrusted to us.

When God makes us new people in Christ Jesus, we become instruments of his redemption and grace in our daily work. Through us the influence of Christ permeates our work environments. And the God who makes *us* new begins to make our workplaces new as well.

Restoration Underway

Jesus went throughout Galilee, teaching in their synagogues, proclaiming the good news of the kingdom, and healing every disease and sickness among the people. News about him spread all over Syria, and people brought to him all who were ill with various diseases, those suffering severe pain, the demon-possessed, those having seizures, and the paralyzed; and he healed them.
—Matthew 4:23-24

When my father got out of the restaurant business, he spent a good deal of time restoring things. He'd buy dilapidated houses, renovate them, and put them back on the market. He'd tackle home renovations—a new kitchen here, a new deck there. Dad especially enjoyed restoring old furniture with the help of my mom, who's a seamstress. They'd pick up an old love seat for twenty bucks at a garage sale, and a couple weeks later you wouldn't recognize it. Dad would refinish the wood. Mom would work on the upholstery. When the restoration was complete you'd think they had just brought it home from the showroom!

The gospels reveal that Jesus loves restoring things too. Not furniture and houses (although he was a carpenter), but people and relationships. In the passage above, Matthew summarizes the heart of Jesus' ministry. If you read through all the gospels you discover that all but one of Jesus' miracles were miracles of restoration—healings, exorcisms, and resurrections. He took people who were broken or distorted or even dead and made them whole again. Jesus' miracles illustrate beautifully and powerfully the meaning of redemption as restoration.

Think about all the effects and distortion of sin in our workplaces. The redemption that comes through Christ's death and resurrection has the power to restore that brokenness. Christ isn't interested in simply protecting us from the dangers and evils of the workplace. He isn't interested in hiding us away from the world. He wants us redeem and restore our workplaces.

And he wants to use us. The One who redeems and restores us sends us out into the world of work as his agents of redemption. In his name and by his power we do what we can to improve conditions in our work settings:

- Where there is tension among coworkers, we seek to be peacemakers.
- Where unhealthy attitudes undermine teamwork, we try to inject a positive and cooperative spirit.
- Where bad work habits diminish productivity, we suggest and model a better way to get things done.
- Where labor and management seem hopelessly separated by an adversarial spirit, we encourage a more cooperative way to resolve differences.
- Where quality or service is lagging, we seek to refocus on service to customers.

Whether our influence is great or modest, we do what we can. We try to restore the work environment to make it look more like God intended it, and in so doing we witness to Christ's redemptive work. We see how big and broad the reach of his redemption is.

In *The Fourth Frontier*, Stephen Graves and Thomas Addington pose this question: "What would happen if 100 million followers of Jesus began to understand what he desires from them at the workplace? Can you imagine the integrity, professionalism, skill, love, forgiveness, service that would come into play?"

Just imagine!

Salt and Light in the Marketplace

"You are the salt of the earth. . . .
You are the light of the world. . . ."
—*Matthew 5:13a, 14a*

Years ago the founders of the Christian Labour Association of Canada (CLAC) surveyed the labor landscape and saw that it was pretty dark territory. As in the States, secular labor unions in Canada wield significant power. At times they assume a militant stance, and their tactics can be ethically questionable. For the most part they square off against management in the posture of an adversary.

For over fifty years CLAC has ventured into that dark territory to organize workers on the basis of principles of honesty, integrity, cooperative negotiation, and fair play. Rather than approaching management as "the enemy," they strive to identify shared values, mutual interest, and win-win solutions. Their agents don't negotiate with Bible in hand, but they do their best to translate kingdom values into workable strategies for the labor world.

CLAC is still a David in the midst of the secular union Goliaths, but it has made impressive inroads into that unfriendly region. In fact, the world of organized labor in Canada is not as dark as it used to be—thanks to the light radiating from the workplace witness of CLAC. And thanks to the salty influence of CLAC holding back the process of decay, the relationship between labor and management hasn't deteriorated as much as it might have.

In the Sermon on the Mount Jesus looked out at the crowd of ordinary men and women and children sitting before him on the mountainside and announced, "You are the salt of the earth." These days we use salt primarily as a seasoning, but in Jesus' day people rubbed salt into meat to hold back the process of decay. It was a preservative. As disciples living by the values of Jesus' kingdom, we're called to act as a preservative holding back the decay of sin in the world. Jesus rubs us into every area of life, including the workplace, to do our salty work.

"You are the light of the world," Jesus continued. Our light shines not only when we share the gospel with neighbors near and far, but also when we behave in countercultural ways that show we live for a different Lord and by a different set of values. Notice that Jesus goes on to say that we must let our light shine before others "that they may see your good deeds and glorify your Father in heaven" (verse 16). In our workplaces we may have limited opportunities to share the good news of the kingdom in words, but we have many opportunities to share that message through "good deeds"—that is, through the ways we go about our work.

Think about what it says to the people in your workplace when you show yourself to be trustworthy. When you treat colleagues with respect. When you go the extra mile to help. When you consistently keep your language out of the gutter. When you exhibit a good work ethic. When you express care in situations where a coworker is dealing with a personal crisis.

All of these "good deeds" are expressions of the light you reflect as a disciple of Christ. And in work environments where such behavior may be rare, you can be sure your saltiness is also doing its job.

Winning Respect

Make it your ambition to lead a quiet life: You should mind your own business and work with your hands, just as we told you, so that your daily life may win the respect of outsiders. . . .
—1 Thessalonians 4:11-12

Whatever you do, work at it with all your heart, as working for the Lord, not for human masters. . . .
—Colossians 3:23

Gale's True Value Hardware has been a family-owned business in Kalamazoo for decades. It's easy for me to stop there on the way to the office. But it's not convenience that keeps me a loyal customer. There are a couple of "big box" stores just as close I could go to. What attracts me to Gale's is their competence. For a person like me who is "do-it-yourself-challenged," I especially appreciate this quality. I have never met a staff member at this store who could not answer my questions, give me directions, and tell me where to go in the store to find what I need. That's competence!

Who are the people in your workplace who stand out because of their strong work ethic? You can always count on them. They're always prepared to go the extra mile. Ninety-nine times out of a hundred what they do is done very well. You always want them on your team. In *The Monday Connection*, William Diehl calls this the "ministry of competency." He calls it the bedrock foundation of our ministry in the workplace.

In his first letter to the Thessalonians, Paul was addressing a Christian community plagued by idleness. The believers were so preoccupied with anticipation for the return of Christ that some of them just shifted into waiting mode; they figured their daily work didn't matter very much. Paul urged them to be responsible and industrious, "so that your daily life may win the respect of outsiders."

Those days, the Greek culture had little use for manual labor. It wasn't for "respectable" people. And in our own culture, many people view not only manual labor but all labor as a necessary evil. The result is that many workplaces suffer from diminished productivity. A 2005 survey, for example, found that the average American worker wastes two hours and five minutes a day, which adds up to $759 billion a year in lost productivity. Web surfing and workplace socializing are the prime culprits. Absenteeism and lateness costs the United States and Canadian economies over $100 billion a year.

These dismal figures can help us appreciate the redemptive value of a ministry of competency in our daily work. Such competence reflects our perfectly competent God. "Whatever you do," Paul urged the Colossian Christians, "work at it with all your heart, as working for the Lord."

Competence. Diligence. A strong work ethic. These attributes catch the attention of coworkers and win their respect. They help improve conditions in the workplace. Most important, they are redemptive because they help restore the workplace to what God intends it to be.

Who are the people in your workplace who stand out because of their competency? Are you one of them?

The Best Place to Meet Jesus

So [Jesus] came to a town in Samaria called Sychar. . . .
Jacob's well was there, and Jesus, tired as he was from the journey,
sat down by the well. . . . When a Samaritan woman came to
draw water, Jesus said to her, "Will you give me a drink?"
—John 4:5-7

Our church has been offering an evangelistic course called "Alpha" for several years. It attracts people who are spiritually curious or searching and gives us the opportunity to introduce or reintroduce Jesus to these folks.

How do these people know about our Alpha program? Members of the church tell them about it and invite them to attend. We are pleased regardless of the number of guests who attend, but we're thrilled if there are more than ten people.

Let's put that into perspective. Over three hundred people attend worship in my church each Sunday. If a quarter of these regular attenders were to invite a friend or coworker or classmate to Alpha, that would be seventy-five people invited. If each of those people were to invite two people, that would be one hundred fifty invited. We're pleased if ten say yes!

Alpha is a great place to meet Jesus. But it's not the *best* place. The best place for most people to meet Jesus is the workplace. Think about it. We encourage over three hundred people to invite someone to come to Alpha to give us the opportunity to introduce them to Jesus Christ. Maybe ten guests show up. But the majority of those three hundred worshipers head into the workplace every week. Some work in settings with a few people around them. Others work for large companies with hundreds or even thousands of employees.

People often let down their guard at work, exposing their vulnerabilities and hurts and frustrations. So that's the place where Jesus wants to meet them. Reading through the gospels we discover that Jesus would meet hurting people wherever they were.

We see this in the story of Jesus' encounter with the Samaritan woman in John 4. You could read the story and say, "What a coincidence! Jesus just happened to sit at that well. And this woman just happened to come by for water at high noon (although drawing water was usually an evening task). So this woman with a stained background just happened to meet the Savior, a very rare Jewish male who would actually talk to a woman in public. And he just happened to take an interest in her life and just happened to have what she needed most—living water."

But we know that Jesus was strategic and purposeful. He took the initiative of putting himself in a position to intersect this woman's life. He created the opportunity for the exchange. He expressed an interest in her life. And in the end he offered her living water that would change her life forever. There was nothing coincidental or accidental about this encounter.

Every day you and I head back into the workplace. I wonder how many "Samaritan women" we meet along the way—in the lunchroom, in the next cubicle, on our team: coworkers, employers, employees, clients, customers, vendors. . . . Many of these people do not and perhaps will not come to church. So they won't meet Jesus there.

But they can meet Jesus in us! We are Christ's presence in our workplaces. We have the opportunity to be the eyes, heart, ears, and hands of Jesus as we take an interest in the people around us, responding to their hurts and concerns and listening to their stories.

Redemption reaches into the brokenness of the workplace in many ways. Surely one of the most valuable is making the presence of Christ tangible in our relationships with our coworkers, customers, and employers.

Discussion Guide

Opening *(5 minutes)*

All of us have experienced our share of indifferent, incompetent, or even hostile service at the mall or the bank or the grocery store. But let's begin on a positive note by sharing a story about someone in the marketplace or workplace who was exceptionally helpful or competent or gracious. What impact did this person have?

Bible Study *(15 minutes)*

Read and discuss the following passage, using the questions to guide your discussion.

- Romans 12:14-21

  Note that these verses are part of a larger teaching section that begins with verse 9, which sounds the keynote to the whole passage: "Love must be sincere. Hate what is evil; cling to what is good." In verses 10-13 the apostle Paul focuses on what love looks like among believers. In verses 14-21 he shifts his focus to our relationship with those outside the Christian fellowship.

One of the ways we can "improve conditions" and bring a redemptive influence to our workplaces is by bringing Christlike love. Pause after each verse to briefly discuss how you might apply that teaching to your daily work. If you don't have time to discuss each verse, consider finishing this study on your own at home.

verse 14:

verse 15:

verse 16:

verse 17:

verse 18:

verses 19-20:

verse 21:

Case Study (15 minutes)

Have someone read the case aloud. Then discuss the questions that follow.

A Complicated Mess

Tom was beginning to regret this promotion. It had been several weeks since he'd been appointed to manage the accounting department. He knew there were problems, but he had no idea just how extensive those problems were. His predecessor had resigned when accounting irregularities came to light. Initially his supervisor suspected carelessness. Now Tom was convinced that the problem was much more serious. Not only were the irregularities more extensive, they were intentional. Tom's predecessor had overstated earnings for several years but the new parent company had not detected the deception. To make matters worse, Tom's new boss was a personal friend of the former employee. Tom couldn't help wondering if she also was involved in the deceptive behavior.

Now he had to decide what to do. Should he trust his boss and report his suspicions to her? Or should he go around her in case she was involved, and inform the parent company? Could he be caught in the middle and find himself in hot water, perhaps even legally? Could his own job be on the line? Maybe, Tom thought, he should just keep his mouth shut, since no one else had detected the extent of the problem, and maybe no one ever would. Maybe he should wash his hands of the whole mess and walk away.

It didn't take long for Tom to eliminate the last option. His integrity wouldn't allow him to walk away or keep quiet. But that didn't make it any easier to figure out what he *should* do as a follower of Christ.

Considering all that is broken and tainted by sin in this situation, what would redemption look like in this scenario? What needs to be "restored" and what might that "restoration" look like?

What steps do you think Tom could take in his position to act redemptively as a Christian in the workplace?

Discussion *(20 minutes)*

1. In your own work setting, what do you think cries out the most for "restoration"?

2. How can you act as an instrument of Christ's redemption in your workplace? In other words, what could you do (or have you already done) to improve conditions in your workplace? (See Day 2 and Day 3 for some general suggestions.)

3. How can "competence, diligence, and a strong work ethic" have redemptive value in the workplace when these are desirable qualities for all workers, Christian or not?

4. "All of us have the potential for a Christian ministry of presence because we interact with others on a daily basis. In fact, people who work from 8:00 a.m. to 5:00 p.m. generally spend more of their waking hours with their workplace associates than with their families" (William E. Diehl, *The Monday Connection*). Describe a time when you were able to bring a "ministry of presence" to someone in your daily work. In what way were you able to be the presence of Jesus to this person?

5. Many churches observe "Mission Emphasis Week" (or Sunday). These wonderful events usually motivate people to support evangelistic outreach nearby or around the world. But as we have seen in this week's readings, the mission of God is broader than evangelism. God has a mission in the marketplace as well. Whether or not your church has a "Mission Emphasis" event each year, share ideas about how your church could do more to remind members of their important mission in the workplace. How could your church encourage members to be a witness in their daily work? You may want to write these ideas down and share them with your church's pastor(s) or council.

Closing *(5-10 minutes)*

If there's time, have each person in the group share a helpful comment or encouraging suggestion from the readings or today's discussion that they will attempt to take with them into their workplace this week.

In your closing prayer, include a strong note of praise for Christ's saving power that transforms even our workplaces. Ask him to use each person in your group as an instrument of restoration and redemption at work in the coming week.

Action Options

Choose one of the following suggestions for extending the session into the week ahead:

Option 1

In the coming week begin each workday by focusing on one condition in your workplace (or in *you* as a worker) that you will try to improve with Christ's help. Ask God to empower and use you to influence positive change that day. At the end of the day reflect on what happened. Give thanks for even small steps of improvement. Or, if you're dealing with one big challenge at work, let that be your focus for the entire week. Think in terms of small steps that can begin to change things for the better. Remember that it is the power of the Holy Spirit that can make this happen.

Option 2

Think of the people you work with or for who make a positive influence at your workplace, regardless of whether they are Christians or not. Make it a point in the coming week to thank them for making a difference.

Option 3

Take a few moments to reflect on how you carry out your daily work. What are your strengths and areas of competence? How would you measure your work ethic? Give thanks to God for the positive and redemptive influence you bring to your workplace and ask for the Holy Spirit's power to make improvements.

Option 4

Think about the people with whom you interact at work. Is there someone for whom life or work is particularly difficult or who may be going through a tough time at home? Prayerfully consider how you might bring a ministry of presence to that person this week—a listening ear, a word of support, or a note of encouragement.

What Is God Calling Me to Do?

"What Is God's Will for My Life?"

He has shown all you people what is good. And what
does the LORD require of you? To act justly and to
love mercy and to walk humbly with your God.

—Micah 6:8

Jesus replied: "'Love the Lord your God with all
your heart and with all your soul and with all your mind.'
This is the first and greatest commandment.
And the second is like it: 'Love your neighbor as yourself.'"

—Matthew 22:37-39

We met at a coffee shop. I figured Derek wanted to tell me about his plans or job opportunities. I was wrong. Derek had worked hard and finished college with a strong GPA. Nobody questioned his potential. But now he wasn't sure at all about the field he had chosen. He was just going through the motions with job applications, almost hoping none of them would pan out. He wondered if pushing his way through college had been a huge and very expensive mistake. "Here I am with a degree," he said, "and I have no idea what God wants me to do with my life."

Choosing a career is one of the biggest decisions a person will ever make. A few people seem to make the decision with ease. They've known since they were ten years old that they want to be a teacher or a farmer. But many others, like Derek, are unsure about what direction they should go. Or they find themselves stuck in jobs that give them little sense of fulfillment. Or after twenty years on the job, they're let go, and wonder what to do next. Still others reach the age of retirement with a sense of dread: "Now what am I going to do with myself?"

And then there's the whole question of God's will. What is God calling me to do? Where is God leading me? Wrestling with these questions can produce a genuine struggle of faith.

For this final week of our study, we'll explore this process of discerning God's will. What questions should we be asking? What considerations do we need to weigh?

Let's begin with a basic insight that connects with what we learned in Week 1: *vocation* precedes *occupation*. Our calling to follow Christ comes *before* our calling to pursue a specific career. The Puritans made a helpful distinction between "general" (corporate) calling and "particular" (individual) calling. The general call refers to the call of the gospel to follow Jesus. It's a calling all Christians share. The Scripture passages from Micah and Matthew have to do with our general calling. They speak of what God calls all of us to do all the time—to pursue justice and mercy, to love God and neighbor.

In addition to that general call all Christians share, we have a "particular" calling to a specific occupation. This particular calling, as Derek discovered, is often hard to figure out. If that's true for you too, I'll say to you what I've said to Derek and to many others: Don't lose sight of your general calling while you're trying to figure out your particular calling. Our eternal future depends on our response to God's call to love and serve him—*not* on our career choice, as significant as that is.

Even if you are biding your time in a short-term job, you're called to carry it out in a way that shows your love for God and neighbor.

A Question of Gifts

Each of you should use whatever gift you have received to serve others, as faithful stewards of God's grace in its various forms.
—1 Peter 4:10

"Again, it will be like a man going on a journey, who called his servants and entrusted his wealth to them. To one he gave five bags of gold, to another two bags, and to another one bag, each according to his ability."
—Matthew 25:14-15

I have a "Herman" cartoon in my workplace collection. Herman is conducting a job interview. His imposing figure is seated at the desk in the foreground. Across the desk a man's head is peeking out from behind an empty chair. Herman is reading the man's résumé—"Your job application says you like meeting the public." People are not always realistic about their own gifts.

When it comes to discerning your particular calling to a job or career, the first thing to do is ask yourself, What gifts or abilities has God given me? Answering that question honestly is often difficult and sometimes agonizing.

Years ago I left a church with over 800 members and accepted a call to one that had about 150 members. Although I loved being pastor at that first church, it was a very demanding situation, and I felt ready to serve a smaller church. I looked forward to a more reasonable pace and the opportunity to write and pursue graduate studies. Over the next few years, in my late thirties, I made a painful discovery. I learned that it takes a special set of gifts and a certain temperament to serve a small church effectively, and that I didn't have either. God wired me to thrive on teamwork and teambuilding. I love the synergy of working with others.

So when I began working in my current large church, I rediscovered the joy and passion of ministry. In Peter's words, I am able to "use the gift(s) God has given me to serve others." I've discovered the task that the master has entrusted to me "according to [my] ability."

Coming to that discovery, however, was not easy. Perhaps that's true for you too, especially if you happen to be right in the middle of that discovery process. As Lee Hardy observes in *The Fabric of This World*, "we were not born with job descriptions taped to our backs." Discovering our particular gifts and aptitudes can take time, for some more than for others.

So what's involved in that process? Hardy suggests four elements:

- *Reflect on past experience.* Think of tasks or projects you have accomplished. What skills did you use or learn? What areas of knowledge did you develop? In what kinds of settings did you work best? What did you learn about working with others?

- *Remain open to future experience.* My experience in a smaller church taught me some valuable lessons about myself that I simply didn't know before. Sometimes it takes trial and error to figure out our particular skills and strengths. It's inconvenient, but it's not the end of the world if you test the waters with one career path and discover that you should be on another one.

- *Consider vocational counseling and testing.* It may not give you the clarity you desire, but the right kind of testing can certainly help.

- *Seek the advice of others who show good judgment.* These must be people who are mature and who will speak the truth to you. Ask how they see you. What do they see as your aptitudes? Can they picture you being effective in the career path(s) you are considering?

Here's a final caution regarding this process of figuring out your gifts. Don't assume that there is only one "right job" for you. All of us have a range of abilities that qualify us to do a number of things. And each one of those options gives us the opportunity to serve God and others.

Discerning our gifts is the first step in choosing an occupation, but it's not the only step. In the following readings we will consider other questions to ask that can help to narrow the field.

A Question of Need

Each of you should use whatever gift you have received to serve others, as faithful stewards of God's grace in its various forms.

—1 Peter 4:10

You have to wonder why someone would *choose* to begin her teaching career in the Baltimore Public School system. It's one of the toughest in the United States. Bethany certainly had other options when she graduated. She could have gone just about anywhere in the country. So why Baltimore? In a word, *need*. It's a school system that has eaten up and spit out some very fine educators over the years. It's rough and tough and profoundly challenging. Bethany found that compelling. She wanted to make a positive difference in the lives of kids who had lots of strikes against them.

Yesterday's reading talked about the first step for discerning your particular calling to a career: asking the "gifts" question. Today we'll focus on the next step: the "needs" question. Once you're aware of which gifts you've been given, you'll need to ask which career path gives you the best opportunity to meet people's needs, and where you might go to pursue your chosen career in order to best serve God and others.

As with the gifts question, the needs question can be difficult to answer. Several factors make it complicated.

First, the cultural values that surround us reinforce a "me first" mentality. Our culture encourages us to make choices on the basis of pay scale, benefits, and opportunities for personal advancement. Often the needs question is not even on the radar.

Another complicating factor is our own sinful condition. Let's face it. This world offers many things that we would love to enjoy. "When it comes right down to it, what I really want out of a job is enough money to buy that five-bedroom Tudor with a private pool, a couple of Swedish cars replete with fifty-watt compact-disc stereo systems, a cottage on the lake, and an annual winter trek to the Bahamas—all required equipment for the good life as it is so vividly set forth in TV commercials and magazine advertisements" (Lee Hardy, *The Fabric of This World*). And beyond the salary and benefits, we also want satisfying jobs. That's understandable, but should job satisfaction be the deciding factor when choosing a job or career? How pure are our motives when making job decisions?

Finally, there's what we might call the "gray-zone" factor. Discerning where need is the greatest isn't easy. A Christian physician may choose to go to Africa to work with AIDS victims, where the need is overwhelming. But she may also choose a research position with a prestigious pharmaceutical company in North America to work on finding a cure for HIV-AIDS. What is the greater need? And how do I balance the needs of my individual or family circumstances with the needs of others?

These are challenging questions to ask and to answer. But the Bible requires us to ask them. "Each of you must use whatever gift you have received *to serve others*," says Peter. And Paul calls us to "do something useful with [your] own hands, *that [you] may have something to share with those in need*" (Eph. 4:28).

How well does your work enable you to serve others and meet their needs?

A Question of Passion

They said to [Nehemiah], "Those who survived the exile and are back in the province are in great trouble and disgrace. The wall of Jerusalem is broken down, and its gates have been burned with fire." When I heard these things, I sat down and wept. For some days I mourned and fasted and prayed before the God of heaven.
—Nehemiah 1:3-4

In exile, Nehemiah was a cupbearer for King Artaxerxes of Persia. When he heard about the plight of his Jewish people back in Judah and how the walls of Jerusalem lay in rubble, Nehemiah was moved to tears. He poured out his heart before God with fasting and prayer. He felt an overwhelming burden to find a way to get back to his homeland and rebuild the walls of Jerusalem. For Nehemiah that burden was a calling from God.

Some time later Nehemiah summoned the courage to ask for permission to return to Jerusalem to rebuild the city. To Nehemiah's amazement the king consented.

This story points to a third question we must ask in the process of discerning God's call to a particular career or occupation. It's the question of *passion*. Has God given you a passion to serve others in a particular way? Do you have a deep concern within you that you can't seem to shake? If so, this may be God's way of pointing you in the direction of a career he wants you to pursue.

In *The Fourth Frontier*, Stephen Addington and Thomas Graves tell the story of author Dianna Booher. In her late twenties Booher was the sole supporter for her two young children and a husband who had mental illness. She'd completed her first year of teaching but couldn't picture herself continuing in education. Instead, she felt a growing passion to develop her gift for writing. As she explored the possibilities, one path seemed best—writing Bible study materials.

For several days Booher went without sleep. Finally she poured out her heart to God: "I don't know what you have for me to do with my life, or how I'm going to support this family. I want to become a writer with all my heart, but I don't see how I can make a living. Lord, you've just got to give me an answer—now. I need sleep." With that she was filled with a sense of peace and a clear sense of calling to be a writer. Booher went on to write more than forty books.

Did passion play a role in helping you decide on a career or occupation? Do you still feel that passion, even if it's ten or twenty or thirty-five years into a career or job? Recognize that what you feel deeply about, whether it's related to your current job or not, has been instilled in you by the God who gave you your gifts and opened your eyes to the needs of others.

Recently I had lunch with a manager for a major corporation. He finds many things about the corporate culture frustrating. But even now, in his mid-fifties, he still feels a passion to bring his Christian values into the workplace to make a difference for his coworkers and employees.

Passion is a signal. So whether you are a newly minted high school or college grad searching for a career path, or you're well along a path you chose long ago, pay attention to that passion deep inside that won't go away. It may be God nudging you in a new direction to accomplish his purposes.

A Question of Opportunity

But Joseph said to [his brothers], "Don't be afraid. Am I in the place of God? You intended to harm me, but God intended it for good to accomplish what is now being done, the saving of many lives."
—Genesis 50:19-20

My mother, now in her eighties, is an avid reader. Whenever she comes to visit she peruses my bookshelves for some new volume she hasn't read yet—a Yancey or Peterson or "Oooh, a new Ortberg." She's in her glory. Over the years she has led Bible studies and given inspirational talks to larger gatherings. Mom loves to write poetry and prose. She's eloquent. And did I mention her painting? She still gives lessons to a few students.

Not bad for a woman who didn't pass her high school equivalency exam until she was a senior citizen! Sometimes we reminisce together about what *might* have been if she'd been born fifty years later. Seminary would have been a feast for her. I remember Mom wondering aloud more than once over the years if she could enroll in a local college and take some English and writing classes. We encouraged her to check it out.

But something always got in the way. A child struggling with addiction. A husband who developed a debilitating illness. Her work as a grandmother, church volunteer, and support for other parents dealing with their kids' addiction. You might say *life* got in the way of other possibilities for my mom.

Mom has the gifts to be in full-time ministry or art or teaching or writing. She knows the needs that could be met with those gifts. She has a deep passion for people who are broken or spiritually lost.

The bottom line is, my mother simply didn't have the *opportunity* to use those gifts and passions in some of the ways she may have preferred or enjoyed. She's not bitter. She understands that she's had plenty of things to do in God's kingdom. She did what she could with the doors that were open (or closed) to her. She made herself available to God, and God used her gifts and passions to meet others' needs in surprising ways.

Maybe you can relate to my mother's experience. Maybe you understand that sometimes the most significant question to ask concerning God's will for your career or occupation is the "opportunity" question: given my particular set of circumstances, what doors are open or closed? Maybe like Joseph, you recognize God's hand directing your paths in ways you may never fully understand.

We could call God's behind-the-scenes directing "the *providence* factor." The Heidelberg Catechism gives a beautiful definition of providence: "The almighty and ever present power of God by which he upholds, as with his hand, heaven and earth and all creatures, and so rules them that leaf and blade, rain and drought, fruitful and lean years, food and drink, health and sickness, prosperity and poverty—all things, in fact, come to us not by chance but from his fatherly hand" (Q&A 27).

These days motivational speakers are apt to say, "Pursue your dreams! You can do anything you set your mind to! The sky's the limit!" But as followers of Christ, we learn to temper our personal ambitions with a healthy reliance on God and the sincere prayer "Your will be done."

So if your grad school applications are all turned down, or that business opportunity falls apart, or you can't accept that position you've waited years to get because your elderly parents need you close by, you can be bitter or angry. You can wonder what you did wrong. Or you can ask the "opportunity" question and contemplate where God's providence may be leading you.

Discussion Guide

Opening *(5 minutes)*

Choose one of the following options to open your session.

Option 1

Describe—in just one or two words—your attitude toward your current occupation or other work.

Option 2

Take turns sharing one insight or comment from this week's readings that you found helpful or encouraging.

Bible Study *(15-20 minutes)*

Part 1: God's "General" Calling

God's "general" calling refers to the things God calls all of us to be and to do, regardless of our specific occupation. Below are some of the many passages in the Bible that express God's "general" calling. Read them slowly and consider what God is calling you to be and do.

- Acts 2:38: "Repent and be baptized, every one of you, in the name of Jesus Christ for the forgiveness of your sins."
- Matthew 22:37, 39: "Love the Lord your God with all your heart and with all your soul and with all your mind.". . . "Love your neighbor as yourself."
- Matthew 6:33: "Seek first [God's] kingdom and his righteousness, and all these things will be given to you as well."
- 1 Peter 4:10: "Each of you should use whatever gift you have received to serve others."

Part 2: God's "Particular" Calling

God's "particular" calling refers to his call to each person to a specific occupation. Read the passages below and answer the questions that follow.

- 1 Corinthians 12:27-31 and Matthew 25:14-30
  The first passage refers specifically to tasks or occupations within the church. The second speaks more generally about the tasks Christ entrusted to his servants before ascending to heaven. In both passages, the task or occupation is based on the same thing. What is it? What differences, if any, do you see between the spiritual "gifts" in the Corinthians passage and the "abilities" of the Matthew passage?

  How do these passages relate to the way we seek to know God's will for our vocational or career choices?

  On the basis of your experience, what are some practical things to keep in mind as you try to discern what abilities or gifts God has given you?

  What advice would you give to someone who has a range of abilities and is qualified to do a number of things? How can this person "narrow the field"?

Case Study *(15 minutes)*

Have someone read the case aloud. Then discuss the questions that follow it. You may want to draw on the reading for Day 5 when discussing the case.

Called to Be a Bricklayer?

With a keen eye, expert hands, and fluid motions, Dale set another brick in place. I stood watching for a few moments and then asked how long he'd been a bricklayer. "Well, let's see." He rested the level on top of the brick to confirm what his eyes already told him. Perfect. "Thirty-nine years. Then I retired. Now I just do small jobs like this. I like helping the college."

"So how did you get into this line of work?" I wondered. Straightening for a moment, he said, "My parents were missionaries. I was visiting relatives in Grand Rapids. I decided to go back home where I had a job waiting for me. My uncle knew of a bricklayer who needed labor. He thought I should give him a call. I did. He offered me $1.85 an hour. That was better than the job I was going home for, so I decided to take it. Spent all those years with the same company! We did most of the buildings around here." He smiled with satisfaction and bent over again.

Then I asked if he thought of his job as a calling. He worked in silence for a moment, obviously weighing his answer. "Not really. I guess I didn't think of it that way. It was a job." He completed another layer of bricks. "Now my brother, he was called to the ministry. Maybe you know him." He offered the name and I did. "He was on the mission field too."

"So do you enjoy your work?" I asked. "Oh, I suppose. Winters around here are long, though. That can be miserable. And then you get this muggy stuff in the summer."

I couldn't help asking if he'd ever thought about what might have happened had he passed on the buck eighty-five job and gone back home. "Nah. Never really thought about it."

We chatted a bit longer. As I walked across campus to my appointment I found myself wondering, When is a job a calling?

Explain why or why not you think that God called Dale to be a bricklayer.

Why do you suppose some Christians feel quite certain about God's calling or leading in their career choice and others do not?

Do you think it would have made any difference for Dale's work if he had seen his job as a calling from God?

Discussion *(15 minutes)*

1. How can you see God's "particular" calling in the work that you do? What difference does that make to you? How can you tell if you are doing what God wants you to do?

2. What were some of the factors that led you to pursue the work you do? What role did the gifts or abilities God gave you play? The desire to serve others in some way? A particular passion? A door that opened (or closed)?

3. Of the four discernment strategies mentioned in Day 2, which, if any, have you found helpful? Take this time to share, on the basis of your collective experience and wisdom, other questions or considerations that are helpful in discerning God's call to a particular career or job.

Alternative Approach

Instead of discussing the three questions above, take turns sharing how this week's readings either confirmed your sense of God's leading to your current work *or* provoked some questions about where or how God may be leading you.

Closing *(5 minutes)*

Take a moment to read and reflect on this statement: "There is a reason why I am who I am, although that reason may not be immediately apparent to me. I was placed here for a purpose, and that purpose is one which I am, in part, to discover, not invent" (Lee Hardy, *The Fabric of This World*).

Then invite each person to share at least one thing you would like the others to remember in prayer about your daily work. This may be a thanksgiving, a frustration, or a passion. Take the time to pray for each person in the group.

Action Options

Choose one of the following suggestions for personal follow-up to today's session:

Option 1

Take time each day in the coming week to call or to write a note of encouragement to someone you know who seems well-placed by God for the job she is doing. Tell the person why you feel that way. This may relate to someone's volunteer ministry at your church or to a person's daily work. Feel free to tell the person what you have been studying and why it made you think of him or her.

Option 2

Take time to list all or some of the people who are served by what you do in your daily work. For the next week use this as a prayer list before or as you head to work. Pray that God will bless the people on your list through what you do that day.

Option 3

If you are uncertain about the career path you've chosen, schedule a visit in the coming week with someone who knows you well whose maturity and judgment you trust. Ask this person to help you by answering these questions:

- What do you see as my strongest gifts or abilities?

- What kinds of tasks do you believe I am most effective at performing?

- How well suited do you think I am for the work that I am doing?

Option 4

Take ten to fifteen minutes to reflect on the things that matter deeply to you—beyond your personal well-being. Which issues or developments in the world at large, in your community, or in your work setting stir a passion? Make a list of these. Beside each one, note the ways you could act on those concerns. Then bring your list to God in prayer. Thank God for laying these concerns on your heart and ask for guidance to act on these concerns in ways that honor God and serve his purposes.

Option 5

Knowing about God's providence helps us in three ways, according to the Heidelberg Catechism: "We can be patient when things go against us, thankful when things go well, and for the future we can have good confidence in our faithful God and Father that nothing will separate us from his love" (Q&A 28). Reflect on how this applies to your daily work and sense of God's leading. Where or how do you feel the need to be patient as you wait on God? In what ways has God blessed and led you? How can you feel confident about your future and the knowledge that this too is in God's hands?